MAKING THINGS WORK

BELLS AND BUZZERS

by

Alex Brinded

KidHaven PUBLISHING

Published in 2019 by KidHaven Publishing, an Imprint of Greenhaven Publishing, LLC
353 3rd Avenue, Suite 255, New York, NY 10010

This edition is published by arrangement with Booklife Publishing.

Written by: Alex Brinded
Edited by: Holly Duhig
Designed by: Gareth Liddington

Cataloging-in-Publication Data

Names: Brinded, Alex.
Title: Bells and buzzers / Alex Brinded.
Description: New York : KidHaven Publishing, 2019. | Series: Making things work | Includes glossary and index.
Identifiers: ISBN 9781534529199 (pbk.) | ISBN 9781534529212 (library bound) | ISBN 9781534529205 (6 pack) | ISBN 9781534529229 (ebook)
Subjects: LCSH: Electric bells--Juvenile literature. | Electricity--Juvenile literature. | Electric motors--Juvenile literature. | Fire prevention--Juvenile literature.

Classification: LCC TK7109.B756 2019 | DDC 621.386--dc23

Printed in the United States of America

CPSIA compliance information: Batch #BW19KL: For further information contact Greenhaven Publishing LLC, New York, New York at 1-844-317-7404.

Photocredits: Abbreviations: l-left, r-right, b-bottom, t-top, c-centre, m-middle. All images are courtesy of Shutterstock.com.
Cover - IgorZD, INattapongl, BrAt82, Margo Harrison, kryzhov, Kittapasp, Robert J. Beyers II, Billion Photos, I love photo, PunkbarbyO, T R A I M A K,Roman Pyshchyk, KobchaiMa, 4 - nadtochiy, 5 - Vietnam Stock Images, 6 - e X p o s e, 7 - Andrey_Popov, 8 - Michkasova Elena, 9 - CCat82, danymages, Sergiy Kuzmin, B.Melo, 10 - Progressfoto, 11 - EStas, 12 - Duplass, 13 - kryzhov, 14 - Sergei Kolesnikov, 15 - ra3rn, 16 - Littlekidmoment, 17 - TungCheung, 18 - Littlekidmoment, 19 - Vlad Bokarev, 20 - Asier Romero, 21 - Africa Studio, 22 - noPPonPat, 23 - Monkey Business Images.

Images are courtesy of Shutterstock.com. With thanks to Getty Images, Thinkstock Photo and iStockphoto.

CONTENTS

Words that look like **this** can be found in the glossary on page 24.

MAKING SOUND

Buzzers and bells all have different sounds. This is because they are usually used to tell us different things. For example, mobile phones sometimes buzz when someone is calling us.

Church bells tell people about church events.

This buzzer allows a patient to call a nurse or doctor.

Electric buzzers and bells are connected to a **circuit**. The buzzer or bell works when electricity flows around the circuit.

BUZZERS BUZZ

Devices that buzz have to be **triggered**. For example, alarm clocks buzz and ring when the hands of the clock reach the time that has been set.

Some buzzers have small **motors** that buzz when they spin. The motor will spin a wheel, which may be attached to a weight. The whole device shakes when it spins really quickly.

Electric toothbrushes buzz because of a spinning motor.

BELLS RING

A bell rings when a clapper strikes it. The clapper is like a hammer. It hits the bell and makes it **vibrate**. Bells can have clappers on the inside or on the outside.

These clappers are on the inside of these bells.

Bike Bell

Hand Bell

Service Bell

Big Bell

TYPES OF BELLS

This clapper is on the outside of the bell.

Some bells are electric and some are **manual**. A bike bell is manual because a cyclist has to press and release a lever for the clapper to strike the bell. Bike bells warn other road users there is a cyclist.

In electric bells, electricity makes the clapper hit the bell. The clapper hits the bell again and again while the electricity flows. The clapper stops when the electricity stops.

DOORBELLS

A doorbell is a type of electric bell. When you press the button on a doorbell, electricity flows through the circuit. This electricity causes a sound to play.

Doorbells can usually be heard all around the house.

In an **apartment** building, each apartment has its own doorbell. The front door for the whole building can be unlocked from inside each apartment.

The person at the door will hear a buzzer sound to let them know they can go in.

TELEPHONES

Old telephones had bells on them, which would ring when someone called. The call triggered the clapper. People say "I'll give you a ring" because telephone bells would ring!

Modern mobile phones buzz when a call or message is received. This buzzing sound is made by a tiny motor turning a weight. The weight is moved very fast, which makes the phone shake.

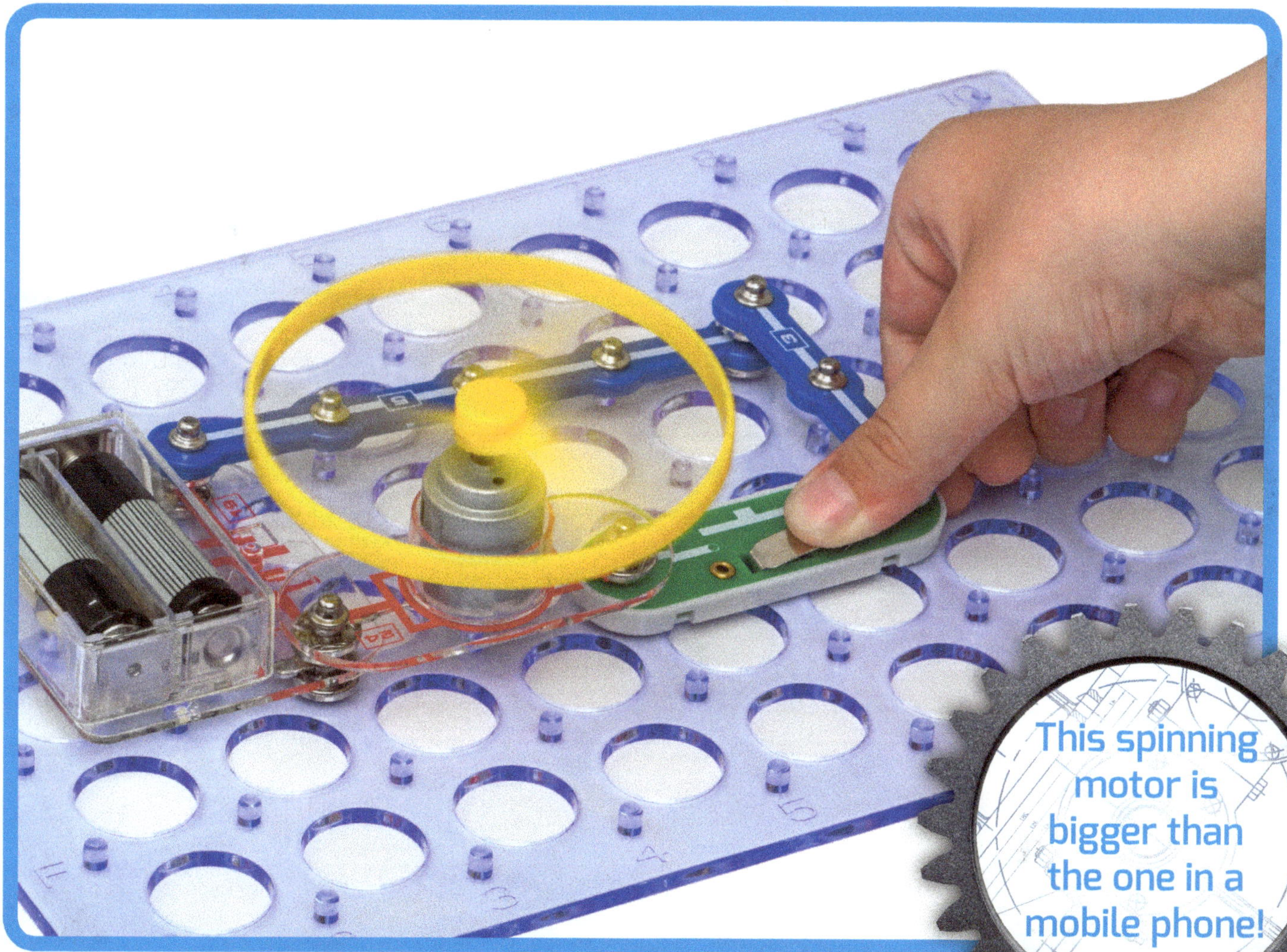

This spinning motor is bigger than the one in a mobile phone!

ALARM BELLS

Fire alarms make a noise when a fire is detected. When a fire alarm sounds, everyone must leave the building safely. Fire alarms can be bells, **sirens**, or horns.

Fire alarms can be triggered by smoke or heat.

Smoke detectors can be found in schools and homes. If there is smoke in the room, the smoke detector makes a loud noise.

The quicker the firefighters can get to the fire, the easier it will be to put it out.

Emergency services have to get to an emergency as quickly as possible. If they hear the alarm bell at the fire station, they have to move fast to get to the emergency in time.

Old fire engines had bells so vehicles would hear them coming and let them pass. Fire engines, police cars, and ambulances now use sirens. Sirens are louder and easier for drivers to hear.

COUNTING DOWN

Timers are clocks that count down and measure time. When they reach zero, an alarm goes off that buzzes or rings to tell you the time is up.

A microwave has a timer that counts down as food or drink is heated. The microwave triggers a bell when the timer reaches zero to tell you that it has finished.

KEEPING TIME

These loudspeakers make the buzzer sound louder.

In sports such as basketball and ice hockey, a loud buzzer marks the end of each **period** of play. This buzzer has to be loud enough for players to hear over the noise of the crowd.

A school bell tells students and teachers when classes start and finish. The sound can be heard throughout the school so that everyone can get to their classes on time.

GLOSSARY

apartment home that is part of a larger building

circuit wires that connect electrical devices together

devices machines that are made for one thing

manual operated by a person

motors machines that change electrical energy into movement

period an amount of time

sirens very loud warning devices

triggered set off

vibrate shake a lot

INDEX